MW01134404

Shining from Within

A 30-Day Devotional for Tween and Teen Girls

written by

JASIYA GREEN

INK To LEAGACY PUBLISHING

Blythewood, SC

Cover Design by Tamell Green
Interior Design by Jasiya Green & Tamell Green
Edited by Tamika Sims & Jason Green

Ink to Legacy Publishing
PO Box 229, Blythewood, SC 29016

SHINING FROM WITHIN: A 30-DAY DEVOTIONAL FOR TWEENS & TEENS
Copyright © 2020 Jasiya Green
Published by Ink to Legacy Publishing
Blythewood, South Carolina 29016

www.ink2legacy.com

ISBN 978-1-7363674-9-0 (hardback)

ISBN 978-1-7363674-4-5 (pbk)

ISBN 978-1-7363674-3-8 (ebook)

Library of Congress Control Number: 2020925369

For the girl reading this:

Hi! I'm Jasiya!
I wrote this devotional because all the topics that I discuss are issues that I have dealt with and are still overcoming with the help of God. Having a relationship with God is essential for being a happy tween/teen because He is always there to help us understand that we're not alone. Not everyone knows how to talk to God or connect with Him because I didn't.

With the help of my family, church family, and books like these, I began to know God for myself. Over the course of these 30 days, I will help you talk to God and build a relationship with Him like you haven't had before.

So here's how this devotional will go: I will tell you a story from my life pertaining to the topic and give you the quote and prayer that helped me get through that hardship in my life. I've sprinkled a few activities throughout also.
Get ready!

Love,

Jasiya

1

au·then·tic

/ôˈTHen(t)ik/ of undisputed origin; genuine

If you're like the average teenager, you may have already created one or more social media accounts. In the modern age, it's pretty much expected of us. From Instagram to TikTok, it seems that everyone who is our age is active on these platforms as early as they can be. But that wasn't the case for me. When I was in sixth grade, I always found myself being with the "popular" kids. It wasn't that I wanted to be popular as well but I always ended up being with them. It made me question myself when I saw them on the social media platforms like Snapchat, Instagram, or Musical.ly, the old version of TikTok. I wasn't allowed to be on any social media because my Mom knows the dangers of social media and didn't want me exposed to that at such a young age. Even though Mom knows best, I still wanted an Instagram account no matter how dangerous she thought it was. Eleven-year-old me thought I had it figured out.

More months went by without me having any social media accounts until my teachers had us do this one assignment for English class. We had to make a Tweet and Instagram post about who our celebrity role model is and why. I told my Mom about it and she thought I was telling a story until I showed her the assignment. My Mom wanted me to make the Tweet and Instagram from her account and at first, I was fine with it but then I had a thought. This could be the day that I get my own social media accounts so I begged and begged for her to say yes. She finally broke and agreed to let me make accounts on Instagram and Twitter! I was so happy and I started setting up my account immediately. Well, I was happy until she said she was going to be signed in to my account on her phone! Now that I look back, I realize she only did it to keep me safe and train me on what to and not to post.

While I originally got the social media accounts for a class assignment, my mom allowed me to keep them. She taught me how to properly use social media and because of this, my feeds don't have anything that doesn't represent me posted in them. My username was "Jojoleads_". People picked at it and thought it was lame and I started to think that too until I realized that I am a leader and my username was very fitting. I started to post things that I loved; Christian quotes, animals, food, stuff like that. I was enjoying doing it and it was because I was being my authentic self and showing others who I am.

That's the importance of being authentic. You should live for yourself and no one else. If you like something that doesn't follow the trends, oh well! Being authentic is even cooler. It's what makes you stand out from the crowd. Never feel out of place for being yourself because being YOU is what you're supposed to do!

Psalm 139:14
"I praise you because I am fearfully and wonderfully made; your works are wonderful, I know that full well."

Dear Lord,
Thank you for setting me apart from others. Even when I don't understand why you set me apart please never allow me to never shy away from it. I want to use my gift(s) to serve you Lord and if that means I have to be different then have your way, Lord. When I want to blend in, help me to remember that I am fearfully and wonderfully made.
Amen.

Mirror Reflection

The Process to Being Authentic on Social Media:

1. Embrace who you are
2. Post things you like
3. Introduce your friends to things you like to help them embrace your interests

You Are Not Alone
Isaiah 41:10

a·lone
/ə'lōn/ having no one else present

I'm not talking about not having friends around at the moment alone. I'm talking about feeling like you're the only person that's going through something alone. Feeling that kind of alone sucks. A time where I felt alone was when my parents split up when I was nine. I am a daddy's girl, and when my dad abruptly left my home, it hurt. All my friends' dads were still living in their homes and I felt jealous about that. I would see how happy they'd be when their dad would come to pick them up from school and I missed having that. I began to shut the world out while not talking to my friends, my Mom or Dad, or any of my family about my feelings and bottling everything up. It wasn't a great feeling at all and I felt like being the only cocoa puff left in the cereal bowl. Have you ever felt that alone?

One thing that helped me to not feel alone was going through therapy as a family. The therapist helped me to voice my opinions and feelings with my parents again, which made me not feel as alone. Being able to explain my feelings to someone that doesn't even know me was comforting for me. Oftentimes, it helped to talk with my therapist alone.

Isaiah 41:10
"So do not fear, for I am with you; do not be dismayed, for I am your God. I will strengthen you and help you; I will uphold you with my righteous right hand."

The Lord says, "So do not fear, for I am with you." He will comfort you when you feel alone. He will always be there for you no matter what you're going through. So when you feel alone, call on the Lord. He will always be there. Even when you feel alone, you aren't alone. Being intentional about feeling better always helps. I get my phone and blast my Gospel playlist. Gospel music always brings me a sense of peace especially when I feel like I'm really connecting with God.

Here is the prayer that I started praying whenever I felt alone and the prayer that you can use when you feel alone:

Dear Heavenly Father,
Please forgive me for overlooking my friends who feel alone. Help me to be a shoulder for others to cry on when they feel alone. Lord if I have abandoned someone to where they feel alone please forgive me. Thank you, Lord, for being here to hear my cries. Thank you for what you have done in my life. I ask that you help all of the other people that feel alone find peace in their time of darkness. Father, whenever I feel alone again, please help me to be delivered from that place of darkness.

Mirror Reflection

When was a time that you can remember feeling alone? What happened to make you feel this way?

_____

_____

_____

How did you overcome feeling alone? If you haven't overcome yet, what are some things that you are doing to work towards overcoming feeling alone?

_____

_____

_____

Find your top five Gospel songs and add them to a playlist. Take a few minutes each day (10-20) to give God praise and spend intentional time with Him.

_____

_____

_____

_____

_____

 Scan this QR code to be taken to my list of my favorite Gospel songs!

hap·pi·ness

/ˈhapēnəs/ the state of being happy

Many things can make us feel happy, whether they big or small. Happiness is our choice and we decide which emotional path to take each day we wake up. Piggybacking off of the example that I used in the last devotional, (you know, the one where my parents split), one day I heard a knock on the door, and guess what? After two years of my dad being out of the house, but still very present in my life, my parents decided to bring our family back together. My Dad finally moved back in. I burst into tears… tears of joy of course. My best friend was finally back! This was a big thing to be happy about. I instantly forgot about having to split my time between two homes over the course of the two years while he was away. I could finally be happy again. I felt like my puzzle was now complete.

We had Daddy-Daughter Day outings, Facetime calls, and many other moments, but nothing beats hearing my Daddy snore right in our own home or see him fall asleep on the couch after a hard day's work. One of my favorite things to hear is when my Dad makes my Mom laugh so hard. She loves to laugh. He is a low-key comedian. When my Dad came back, that made me realize that I should enjoy the small things in life as well. I allowed myself to be sad for two years because my Dad was out of the house when many girls may not even have their Dad in their lives at all. Though his body wasn't physically present all the time, I know that his love was. If you can't already tell...my family is important to me. They all are my happy place.

There were many other things I could have been happy about. I could have been happy about the business that I started during that time, the book that my sister wrote, or the strong relationship me and my mom built. Sometimes we only focus on what makes us sad, causing us to dwell on feeling sad. I've learned that celebrating every small thing that makes you happy can help you find joy in life. Once I realized that there were many things I could have been happy about, I felt convicted. I only focused on the bad things that were going on in my life rather than focusing on the many miracles and blessings God had given me. I felt like I had been ungrateful and greedy. When you feel sad and you want to feel better, think of all the blessings and good things God has done for you.

Psalm 30:11
"You turned my wailing into dancing; you removed my sackcloth and clothed me with joy."

"You have turned my wailing into dancing." Find the happiness in the small things girl! Don't waste time being sad when there are many things to celebrate! You only live one life so don't waste it dwelling on things that make your life sad or miserable. Have fun while you're young and you have the time to have fun.

Here is the prayer that I started praying whenever I wanted to ask God to help me find the good in the bad, and the prayer that you should use when you want to find the good in the bad:

Dear Loving Father,
Please forgive me for never minding the small things you've blessed me with. Help me to be grateful for the things I have even when I want more. Thank you, Lord, for the many blessings you've given me. Thank you for allowing me to have things to be happy about even in my times of sadness. Thank you for what you have done and the things you will do in my life. I ask that you help all of the other people that are struggling to be happy. Father, whenever they feel sad please remind them of all the things they have to be happy about. Remind them that they got to wake up to live another day.
Remind them of how great you are Lord.
In Your Holy Name, I pray,
Amen.

Mirror Reflection

List the big or small things you find happiness in:

_____

_____

_____

When were you in a situation where you felt so sad that you felt like you couldn't find the good in the bad? Write the good things down so that when you think of that bad thing, the good will outweigh the bad.

_____

_____

_____

Three Ways to Find Your Happiness:

1. Make friends
2. Find a hobby
3. Get involved in your church (i.e. Joining the choir, volunteering)

Word Search

GOD   GIRL   PRAY   AUTHENTIC

LIGHT   LOVE   GOALS   MIRROR

FRIEND   FORGIVE   ANXIETY   SHINING

LOOK UP, DOWN, & ACROSS FOR THESE WORDS

A	Z	G	C	U	G	B	G	O	D
N	K	O	J	S	I	P	K	C	F
X	T	A	D	F	R	I	E	N	D
I	M	L	E	O	L	N	C	J	B
E	C	S	V	R	B	H	H	P	M
T	H	D	O	G	E	K	D	R	I
Y	K	J	L	I	G	H	T	A	R
Z	F	M	U	V	C	F	Z	Y	R
A	U	T	H	E	N	T	I	C	O
S	H	I	N	I	N	G	O	X	R

13

Day 4

Feeling Sad

John 16:33

sad

/sad/ feeling or showing sorrow; unhappy

Sadness is one of the worst emotions that there are on
this earth because one thing can make you sad and
ruin your whole day. There is this one time that I can
remember feeling complete sadness. It was when I was in
seventh grade. I mention complete sadness because this
situation truly hurt me.

I had been hanging with a group of girls that were a bad
influence on me. I wasn't using my own voice to make
good decisions. One day, they all ganged up on me and
started picking on me. They called me mean words saying I
was, "lame" and I didn't do bad things. I'm not going to lie,
as much as I acted like those things didn't hurt me, they
did. I was only being my true self and I was getting picked
on for it. People that I thought were my real friends had
turned on me. I went home and I cried and cried. I felt so
terrible. I felt alone like I had no one to lean on.

I didn't want to tell my parents because I didn't want to
get them involved with my teenage drama. Of course, I had
God to lean on but at such a young age, I never knew how
to talk to Him on my own besides saying my prayers at
night and at church. I knew that I needed to start
somewhere in healing from this hurt through the love of

God. I went on Google and searched "Bible verses for when you're feeling sad." Many verses came up but there was one that stuck with me.

John 16:33
"I have told you these things, so that in me you may have peace. In this world, you will have trouble. But take heart! I have overcome the world."

"In this world, you will have trouble," is what stuck out the most. I was DEFINITELY having trouble! I began talking to God about how I felt, holding nothing back. The best thing about talking to God is that He already knows what you're thinking so even if you don't know how to tell Him or even what to tell Him, He knows how to help you overcome what's going on. I started praying. It was a selfish prayer. I only asked God to help me, bless me, and heal me. I wasn't concerned about my "friends." The week that everything happened, the Bible study lessons at church were about overcoming problems. See what I mean? God will help you intentionally and it will surprise you! I left Bible Study with a song in my heart to help me move past the sad moment.

That Bible study lesson helped me feel better about the situation but of course, you don't just magically get over something as it takes time. The next day at school, I walked into class and I decided that I was going to keep walking in my truth, even if that meant being called "lame." Girls remember when God has set you apart from others and lets your light shine so brightly, as there is no hiding it. It took me a long time to realize this. No matter how quiet I tried to be in class, or how much I tried to hide, God or my parents wouldn't allow it, and I thank Him for that. Be glad that you're different! You're you! And you are AMAZING! It doesn't make you better than anyone else because God has given us all a light to shine. Everyone doesn't choose to shine their God-given light. Don't be afraid to shine and don't allow anyone to dim your light. Not even YOU!

I knew that it was nothing but God that the lesson in Bible study was about overcoming problems because I had been praying to feel better about my "friends" treating me the way they had. In Bible study, I learned how to say a prayer in five steps that take selfishness away. First, praise God for who He is. Secondly, confess your sins. Third, thank God. Fourth, pray for others. Fifth, pray for yourself.

Here is the prayer that I started praying whenever I feel sad. You're welcome to use this prayer when you feel sad:

Dear almighty God,
Thank you for loving me at all times. Please forgive me if I've made anyone feel sad intentionally or unintentionally. Thank you, God, for the people that I have that make me feel a bit better when I'm sad. Lord, please help all of the other people that are praying to feel better from sadness. Father, please help me find peace in you. Please help me to feel happy again. I love you so much Lord, thank you for loving me, in Jesus' name I pray,
Amen.

Mirror Reflection

How do you handle feelings of sadness? Take a few moments to find your go-to Scripture so that the next time you're feeling sad you can repeat it in your mind and in your heart.

_____

_____

_____

Prior to reading this devotional, did you know that some prayers could be selfish? Take a few moments to write your own prayer to help you overcome sadness using the guide below.

How to Say a Prayer in Five Steps

Step 1: Praise God.

Step 2: Confess your sins.

Step 3: Thank God.

Step 4: Pray for others.

Step 5: Pray for yourself.

_____

_____

_____

_____

_____

_____

Finding Yourself

Philippians 4:6

self-dis·cov·er·y

/self dəˈskəv(ə)rē/

the process of acquiring insight into one's
own character

Have you ever looked in a mirror and wondered who the stranger was staring back at you? I have. As a Christian, Jesus makes it clear that the only way for us to "find ourselves" is for us to "lose ourselves." This means that our identity cannot be in us, but must be in and with Him.

Identity is defined as the fact of being who or what a person or thing is. Your identity is more than your name; it's your makeup...not that kind of makeup! This kind of makeup is what shows whom you are without having to put it on. It can be your style, the way you talk, or the way you make decisions, which all are part of your makeup. You may be thinking to yourself, what does my makeup look like? Self-discovery is how you find out.

My journey to self-discovery was a long road. When I thought about who I was, I realized I had many titles: Youtube channel host, Daughter, and Big sister. These are all of the titles that I wear but I didn't know who I was separate from the titles that I hold. I thought about that for a long time wondering what I am when I'm not being those things. I honestly didn't know. I found out who I was by spending time with God… lots and lots of time. I'd ask Him to reveal to me what my purpose is and who I really am. He put many opportunities forth for me to figure out whom I was like getting accepted into an international student organization recognized by the U.S. Department of Education and the Health Science Education (HSE) Division of ACTE (HOSA) and many other school programs. For a while, I shied away from who I really am because I was afraid that people wouldn't like my makeup. One thing I had to realize is the makeup that God gives you doesn't change and you can't just wipe it off with makeup remover! You have to live in your God-given truth. Back to what I said earlier about Jesus making it clear that the only way for us to "find ourselves" is for us to "lose ourselves"... I didn't say the journey would be easy. When He put opportunities right in my lap, I was sometimes scared to take them, even though I knew it was God trying to help me find myself. Speaking opportunities helped me discover my love for public speaking. On your self-discovery journey, you will find out a lot of things about yourself that will surprise you.

As tween and teen girls, we experience a lot of changes and challenges on our road to growing up. Making sure you know what your makeup is will help you get through them.

Philippians 4:6
"Do not be anxious about anything, but in every situation, by prayer and petition, with thanksgiving, present your requests to God."

Dear Heavenly Father,
Please reveal to me who I really am. Thank you for making me
fearfully and wonderfully. Please let my self-discovery journey
get me to a destination where my image reflects you. Lord I
know I'm not perfect and I never will be but please make me
like You, O God.
In Your name I pray, Amen.

Mirror Reflection

Tips for Self Discovery:

1. **Listen out for God.** God's voice is heard when you listen to him. He won't just make things apparent and fall in place, you have to listen out for him and go through the steps necessary to your journey.
2. **Don't be afraid to take opportunities** that are handed to you. If you don't really like doing something because you are afraid to but you get a big opportunity to do it, take it. It's one of those things that God is revealing to you from your prayers.
3. **Be ready** for the drastic changes that will happen. When God reveals certain things to you and makes it very apparent, be ready to make changes to your life and be ready to embrace your self-discoveries.

con·fi·dence

/'känfədəns/

a feeling of self-assurance arising from one's
appreciation of one's own abilities or qualities

I 'm afraid of lots of things: heights, spiders, the dark, static electricity, failure, awkward silences, and feeling ugly.

Confidence is a topic I still struggle with today. Sometimes I don't feel confident in my looks and sometimes I don't feel confident when pushing my inner self to keep going. It sometimes is an everyday struggle for me. Learning to like yourself is really hard sometimes. You can watch your friends on Facebook and see their profiles and start to think, man I wish my life was more like theirs. It's easy to start comparing what you have and who you are to them and begin to feel like you don't measure up to them.

You might feel like you really stink compared to other people, but that's most likely not the case. Most likely, you're a pretty amazing person. You just have to take some time to think through what is so great about you. Think about it and begin to list the things that make you special. Maybe you really pay attention to those that don't have friends. Perhaps you're good at drawing or math. Find out what it is that is awesome about you and make a list of those things. When you're feeling down, or need a self-esteem boost, you can pull that list out and remind yourself that you're really pretty great!

Jeremiah 17:7
"But blessed is the one who trusts in the Lord, whose confidence is in him."

Dear God,
Please help me to not think of myself as any less than I am, but rather think of myself with sober judgment, in accordance with the faith that you have distributed to me. For just as each of us has one body with many members, and these members do not all have the same function, so in Christ, we, though many, form one body, and each member belongs to all the others. Help me identify my gift, whatever it may be, and use it to your glory.
Amen.

Mirror Reflection

Tips for starting your journey to confidence:

Check your thoughts. Sometimes you are the only reason you don't feel confident because you have beat yourself up so much in your head that now you can't be confident on the outside.

Do a reality check. You have parents, siblings, grandparents, and most importantly God that care about you. So when you think you're all alone and that no one cares, do a reality check and realize that in reality, you have people that care about you.

See yourself the way God sees you. He doesn't see you as a failure, as a loser, or as anything bad you might think you are. He sees you as important. You're so important that if you were the only person in the world he would have sent his son to die just for you.

anx·i·e·ty

/aNGˈzīədē/

a feeling of worry, nervousness, or unease,
typically about an imminent event or
something with an uncertain outcome

I believe that anxiety is something we've all dealt with at some point in our life, whether it's anxiety or you're anxious about a test, getting a shot at the doctor, or performing a solo in a school play. All of these are things I have personally experienced. If you have also had these feelings, don't ever feel alone. There is always someone going through the same thing as you.

One of my greatest forms of anxiety is knowing that I have a doctor's appointment to get a shot. I have been terrified of shots for as long as I can remember. Every time my mom would tell me that she made me an appointment, I'd always get nervous and dwell on the fact that I have to get a shot or two up until the appointment day. My heart would be in my stomach every time I thought about it. I'd feel my hands get sweaty and my legs would start to tremble. I'd try to calm myself by listening to gospel music because that usually helps me calm down but in this case, it didn't work. A time where I felt anxiety was when I was 13, getting my 13-year-old shots. I tried to tell myself things like " Some people have to get shots everyday so be thankful that it's just this one time." That worked for calming my thoughts but as soon as I got to the doctor's office, it was a completely different story. I sat on the table going through the motions we all go through at the doctor. I got my blood pressure taken and that went fine. I got my ears checked and that went fine. Finally, it was time for me to get my shots… how do you think it went? Terrible! I was so nervous and I kept asking the nurse that was going to give me the shot "How is it going to feel?", "Is it going to hurt?", I even asked her to pinch my arm to give me an idea of how it was going to feel. After five minutes of trying to prepare by asking the nurse to give me examples of how it would feel, she tried to just go for it. I tensed up and snatched my arm away. I had to get two people to hold me down: a nurse and my doctor. I got the shots and it hurt but not as bad as I thought it would. I felt like an idiot for acting the way I did about those shots and I swore up and down that I wouldn't do it again.

The next time I had to get my 15-year-old shots… I did it again! There was a long time period in between me getting shots so I forgot how it felt and I built up that whole idea that shots caused agonizing pain. After that appointment, I also said that I wouldn't do it again. A year later, I had to get my 16-year-old shots. I walked into the office not feeling nervous at all. I sat up on the table and still didn't feel nervous. The nurse walked in with the tray of needles and my heart didn't even drop. She prepared my arm by wiping it with an alcohol pad and then she grabbed my arm and gave me the shot. I tensed up but didn't act crazy this time. The shot that I got was a two-part shot so I went back three weeks later to get the second. Guess what?! I just got the shot. No panicking, no crying, nothing but bravery. I looked back at all the times where I was so scared to get the shots and I thought what's so different about me now than then? I realized it was my relationship with God. Now I finally trusted Him as I should. I was closer to him now than I'd ever been in my entire life. It's important for you to remember that God has always been with you and he always will be whether you are experiencing feelings of anxiety or not.

Psalm 34:4
"I sought the Lord, and he answered me; he delivered me from all my fears."

Dear Heavenly Father,
Thank You for always hearing my cries. Thank you for keeping me above water when I feel so small and helpless. I was so afraid to just let my problems and fears go and give them to You but Lord you never fail me. Thank you for all the anxiety spells you have delivered me and my brothers and sisters in Christ from and will continue to deliver me and my brothers and sisters in Christ from. I love you, Lord, you are so mighty, so big, and so strong. In Your Holy Name, I pray,
Amen.

Mirror Reflection

Understanding what gives you anxiety takes courage. Try not to ignore it. Instead, write them down! You will learn:

1. things you can change and/or
2. things you cannot change.

Talk them over with your parents, your pastor, your doctor, and of course God! Whatever you do, don't hide them! You will get through this.

_____

_____

_____

_____

_____

_____

_____

_____

_____

_____

_____

Feeling Guilty

Ephesians 1:7

guilt·y

/ˈgiltē/ conscious of or affected by a feeling of guilt

Having feelings of guilt can eat you alive. Holding in guilt definitely does that to me. A time where I can remember feeling guilty was when I treated my Dad badly because of the separation. Although my Dad was still making an effort to be in my life even though he was out of the house, I wasn't appreciating the effort he was putting in. He came to get me and my siblings as he usually would but this time I wasn't excited to go with him. I didn't want to go with him at all because I wanted him in the same house as me and I wouldn't be satisfied until he was.

We did our normal routine: picked out our outfits and packed our bags the night before. When my Dad came to pick us up, I said I didn't want to go. I saw his whole demeanor change. At that moment, I didn't feel bad. I didn't care if he felt sad because I didn't think he realized how much he'd hurt me. When he left with my brother and sister, my Mom came in and asked me why I didn't want to go. "I don't want to have to do this," I said. I didn't want to go from seeing my Dad every day to only seeing him on the weekends. I went to bed that night still not caring if I had hurt his feelings. That was so selfish of me to do that as I look back on the situation. It was our only time to spend together and I didn't take the opportunity.

The next morning I woke up and had a fun day with my Mom. As we were on our way home, a certain song came on the radio and she said it reminded her of her dad, my angel grandpa. He passed away when my Mom was in her twenties. Hearing her say how much she missed her dad and wished he was here to see her children made me feel bad for what I had done to my Dad. Here, I have my Mom who wishes she could see her dad when she couldn't even if she tried and I'm here not visiting my Dad just because I want him to feel my pain? I felt like I had done something so wrong and you know what that feeling was? Guilt.

Every time I had a quiet moment, what I had done that to my Dad would ring in my head. When my Dad brought my siblings back from their visit, I apologized to him. I told him why I didn't want to go and why I was apologizing. I thought about it even after my Dad accepted my apology. I was feeling so bad about how I treated him. Lots of times we want to hurt others out of emotions but the only person we hurt, in the end, is ourselves. In conclusion, what I've learned from that situation is that you should never act on emotions and take things for granted because there is always someone who wishes they could be in your situation. You can always see the good in any situation if you choose to.

Ephesians 1:7
"In Him, we have redemption through his blood, the forgiveness of sins, in accordance with the riches of God's grace."

Through the sacrificial death of Christ, you are given forgiveness and salvation as a free gift. So when you have feelings of guilt, that is conviction. Ask God for His forgiveness. Don't take Him forgiving us lightly, don't purposely hurt others, and ask God for His forgiveness because then you are abusing His grace.

Here is the prayer that I started praying whenever I feel guilty or convicted.

Dear Heavenly Father,
Please forgive me for the sins I have committed. Please help my intentions be pure with everything I do. Help me heal when my feelings are hurt. Help me lose that feeling of wanting to get others back or wanting to let them feel my pain. Thank you, Lord, for forgiving me. I ask that you help all of the other people who are dealing with feelings of guilt right now. Father, whenever they feel like they want to get back at someone or do something wrong, please help them make the right decision. Let them know how big you are, Lord. Lord, remind them of how great you are Lord, and how you can help them. I love you, Lord. In Your Holy Name, I pray,
Amen.

Mirror Reflection

How do you deal with having guilt?

_____

_____

_____

What things have you done that made you feel guilty?

_____

_____

_____

Getting Rid of Guilt Process:

1. Forgive yourself
2. Talk about it with those you trust
3. Confess to God
4. Let it go

com·fort zone

/'kəmfərt zōn/

a place or situation where one feels safe or at ease and without stress

Stepping out of your comfort zone is not easy. We tend to never want to step out of where we feel comfortable or try new things. This is the place where we feel the safest. It's also the place where we feel most in control. It's kind of like you already know how your life is going to go at the point and that's why it's called your comfort zone! However, when God calls you out of it, what are you supposed to do? As Christians who are growing and trying to find out whom we are, we should desire to have a relationship with Christ where we are continuously striving to grow closer to Him, no matter how comfortable we want to be.

Writing this devotional made me step out of my comfort zone. Ever since I was 13 years old, (I'm 16 at the time this book is being written), I have been planning to write a book. I'd start and then I'd say "I don't think I'm ready." How this would look is I'd start off strong in my thoughts and ideas and be in a good place with God. The moment when I started to stray away from Him is when my thoughts and ideas would be delayed causing a hold on my book.

33

God called me to step out of my comfort zone to help my fellow sisters in Christ. In this, I began to realize that sometimes your greatest moments are hidden behind your greatest fears. Currently, we are living in a global pandemic, the Coronavirus a.k.a COVID-19. During this time, I definitely exercised stepping out of my comfort zone, when I really thoroughly started to write my book. My thoughts and ideas from when I was 13 years old are actually in print now! It's so amazing to me because three years is kind of a long time to keep putting something off. When you find it hard or almost impossible to step out of your comfort zone and be brave, talk to God. It took me three years to step out of my comfort zone and write my book, so don't put a time limit on your ideas that you are scared to act on. Sometimes it does take time.

Honestly, COVID has helped me in a sense. I have been presented with many opportunities and the biggest one being me finishing my book. My lip gloss business started to flourish making the most sales I'd seen since I started my business. I tell you all of this to say sometimes you have to go through something to really get serious. COVID came to the world and changed everyone's lives. I went from being with my cousins every other weekend to not seeing them for months because we had to social distance. Being stuck inside made me go through self-identity things. I really know who I am now because I've spent all this time with myself. I am really reading God's word and learning it so that I'm able to spread it.

When you are going through something and you feel like it will never end, don't give up. Something greater is coming. This too shall pass. You will make it through. Just confide in the Lord, He's got you, sis!

2 Timothy 1:7
"For the Spirit God gave us does not make us timid, but gives us power, love, and self-discipline."

Dear Lord,

Thank you for always reminding me of Your goodness and mercy. Thank you for pulling me through the battles I've won and the battles that I have yet to face. Please help me to be brave when I walk with you. Help me to remember how powerful You are even when I feel so weak and small. Thank you, Lord, for the blessings I have because I was able to walk through my troubles. I ask that you help all of the other people who are struggling with coming out of their comfort zone. Father, whenever I feel too comfortable please remind me that I have more to do... Allow me to remember how brave I am because of You. I love you, Lord. In Your Holy Name, I pray, Amen.

Mirror Reflection

Use this space to write how you would like to step out of your comfort zone within the next 30 days. You can take it a step further by creating a vision board for it. Creating a vision board is so much FUN! You can do it by yourself, with your family, or with friends. If you've never created a vision board before don't worry. The items needed are pretty simple. You will need: magazines, crayons, markers, any scrapbooking items, and whatever else you would like to use to make it as fancy as you'd like to. Use what you write below to help you create your vision board.

What is it that you would like to do within the next 30 days? Be specific.

What are the next steps you need to take in order to achieve this goal?

If you create a vision board I'd LOVE to see it. Please send your picture to info@beyouplust.com. You can also email me to let me know if you were able to step out of your comfort zone!

Mirror Affirmations

Affirming yourself is a great feeling. If you don't know how great you are how do you expect others to know? Take a few moments to write a few awesome things about yourself on the mirror below. Then go to your mirror and say those things out loud to yourself. I know you're awesome. I hope that you know it, too. God does!

Feeling Angry
Proverbs 29:11

an·gry

/ˈaNGgrē/ having a strong feeling of or
showing annoyance, displeasure, or hostility;
full of anger.

Have you ever been so angry that you feel as if you're not yourself? I've been there. It's so easy to get angry but hard to stop, think, and then react. It's easy to let anger get the best of us and cause us to go off, which isn't going to make us feel better. Being angry isn't a sin but how we react when angry can be. Proverbs 15:18 says, "A hot-tempered person stirs up conflict, but the one who is patient calms a quarrel." Giving full vent to our anger doesn't change the situation.

A time when I was super angry was at school when one of my friends stole something from me and lied about it. It was an eraser from the book fair. Yes, it was something so small but I wanted that eraser. I couldn't wait to get home and show my Mom what I bought. As soon as I got home, I dropped my backpack and got my stuff out. I noticed that I was missing something. I knew that she wanted the eraser because she asked me if she could have it right before it went missing. I knew exactly who to look for the next day at school.

I was so upset that she would take something that I bought when I would never do that to her. The next day

38

rolls around and when I see her, I go straight up to her and ask her about the eraser. Of course, she denies taking it, so I didn't pressure her about it, even though I knew the truth. I almost went the whole school day without talking to her until recess. We always played this game on the monkey bars where we would see who could hang upside down the longest. And this day like any other day, I was down for the game. We climbed up the monkey bars and started hanging. About 30 seconds in, my glasses began to slip off of my face… and then they fell. I was bummed that I lost but I usually win anyway! Lol.

I got down to get my glasses but she was still hanging. She begins to flip off the monkey bars and guess what? When she landed, my eraser fell out of her jacket pocket! I knew she took it! I knew I wasn't crazy. I quickly picked it up before she could and confronted her about it. Now, this is the part where my anger turned into a sin.

Remember, being angry isn't a sin but how we react when angry can be. I started yelling at her and saying mean things that I only said out of anger. I told her that she wasn't my friend, to never talk to me again, and forget about playing the monkey bar game at recess because I was done with her. I was so hurt that she would first steal from me and then secondly, lie about it! We went home and I was still angry at her, even though she apologized.

Now that I'm older, I realize that we should forgive people because it is not our place to try to punish them by shutting them out or ignoring them. God doesn't do that to us when we do wrong so we should try our best to be as forgiving as possible. It doesn't mean you have to still be friends, though. Lol!

When you feel angry, think, and breathe before you react. You may say something out of anger that you don't actually mean, so be mindful of that. And I know, it is hard to think before you react when you're angry but think about how you would feel if someone said mean things to you.

Proverbs 29:11
"Fools give full vent to their rage, but the wise bring calm in the end."

Dear Lord,
Please help me think before I speak especially when I am angry. Allow me the chance to express myself in a way that is not embarrassing to me or others. And if I become angry, Lord please show me the path to extend Grace for others as I want it shown to me.
In Your Holy Name, I pray,
Amen.

Mirror Reflections

Remember to think before you react. I know it may be hard, so here's a process to follow when you get angry.

1. Think before you speak.
2. Take a time out.
3. Don't hold a grudge.
4. Practice relaxation skills.

Letting go of Fear

Joshua 1:9

fear

/ˈfir/ to be afraid of someone or something

There are many times when I have felt fear. Nothing gives me fear like a roaring thunderstorm. Don't laugh, but I am terribly afraid of lightning and the loud boom of thunder. I have always been fearful of them since I was a little kid. From the first sight of lightning or the first roar of thunder, I'd instantly get scared and start crying hysterically. Seriously! As I got older, my family would say that I'm "too old to be crying over storms," but when you're genuinely afraid of something, it doesn't matter who or how old you are. To this day, I am still afraid of storms, but not as much as I used to be LOL. I don't cry or get all worked up anymore like I used to before I knew I could cast my worries and fears on God. Now, I pray when a storm comes and just let God do His work.

As a teen, I see the beauty in the storms and rain. The way the lightning lights up the sky. The way the rain hitting the windowpane is soothing enough for you to get a good nap from hearing it. Even though storms can be scary, there's so much beauty in them. That's what we, not only teens but people, have to realize. There's beauty in everything, even the things that make you fearful. If you're scared of spiders, think about how pretty the webs are that they spin. If you're afraid of clowns, think of the way they make kids laugh until their tummies hurt. See, all you have to do is let go of the fear to see the beauty.

One thing about storms is they don't last forever. So while they're going on, you have to push through it and put your faith over fear. This can be real thunderstorms or the storms of life. The enemy tries to make us fear the beauty of everything that God created but God is stronger than him and will deliver us from any and everything. We just have to ask and be willing to do the work it takes to overcome. When you feel scared of something big or small, call on the precious name of The Father. The Lord hears you and He will deliver you from all your troubles and fears. Sometimes we go through things and have fears so that the Lord can reveal something to us or deliver us from something. Be sure you listen to His voice because while He may put a storm in your path as he will always guide you to the rainbow at the end.

Joshua 1:9
"Have I not commanded you? Be strong and courageous. Do not be afraid; do not be discouraged, for the Lord your God will be with you wherever you go."

"Do not be afraid, nor be dismayed, for the Lord your God is with you wherever you go." See girl? Even when you're afraid God's got you! He's the friend that will never leave you. So the next time you feel afraid or fearful take a deep breath and remember Joshua 1:9.

Here is the prayer that I started praying whenever I felt/feel fearful:

Dear Heavenly Father,
Please forgive me for not putting my faith in you when I feel fearful. Help me to be brave Lord. Help me feel when You are near to calm me. Thank you, Lord, for calming me even when I didn't call on Your Name. Thank you in advance for delivering me from my biggest fears. I ask that you help all of the other people when they are afraid. Father, whenever they feel scared please let them feel your spirit. Let them know how big you are, Lord. Let them know how strong you are, Lord. Let them know how mighty you are. Remind them that they will survive this fear Lord, remind them of how great you are Lord. I love you, Lord. In Your Holy Name, I pray,
Amen.

Mirror Reflection

Why do you think we overwhelm ourselves with our racing thoughts rather than calling on the Lord?

_____

_____

_____

How do you handle your fear?

_____

_____

_____

Doodle the words "Let Go of Fear" in the yellow box.

Day 12
Feeling Insecure
Ecclesiastes 3:11

in·se·cure

/insə'kyŏor/ not confident or assured;
uncertain and anxious

Insecurity is one of the ones that I struggled with the most. Growing up in this day and age, the societal beauty standard is to have a "Coke bottle shape," curly hair, and all sorts of other stipulations that are so degrading to girls who don't have those things. Ever since I was in third grade, I had breasts. People would always point them out and it made me feel self-conscious. Not many girls in my class had breasts, so often the ones who didn't have them would make me feel bad about having them, even though it's nothing to be ashamed of. In fourth grade, I was going through a tough time, as you guys have heard lots of stories from this period in my life. The one where my parents were separated for two years is one of those stories. In the beginning, when the separation happened, I was always stressed. Stress can take a toll on your health including your appearance. I would stress eat and I began to gain weight. I was also depressed.

At nine-years-old, I was going through so much, and being picked at for my appearance added on more stress. I would try to not eat for days at a time and wear clothes that weren't so fitting. As I got older, my breasts still grew greatly but I lost the weight. From all of those years of being picked at and having my insecurities pointed out, I began to feel insecure about those things even when I shouldn't have. Over time, I became confident with my body no matter what anyone said. No matter who pointed out my insecurities, I had to stop caring about what other people thought about me.

This is my advice to you: stop caring about what other people think or what other people have to say and love yourself! You only have one life, so don't spend it being self-conscious or insecure. One thing that I've heard throughout my life and it has stuck with me is, "Your body is someone else's dream body." You may not like your thighs or the fact that your belly may be larger than you'd like it to be but girl, be proud of it! That's what I had to realize.

Ecclesiastes 3:11
"He has made everything beautiful in its time. He has also set eternity in the human heart, yet no one can fathom what God has done from beginning to end."

After years of learning to love me for who I am, I started my cosmetics line to help girls get out of that dark place where I so vividly remember being. My mission is to empower girls to shine from within because real beauty comes from within. It doesn't matter how big or small your chest or bottom is, the real beauty will always come from the inside. "He has made everything beautiful in its time." Never forget that. You are made in the image of God so of course, you're beautiful! There is nothing wrong with adding to our appearance because God does want us to take care of our temple. But if we focus on our inner beauty, the outer beauty will take care of itself. My Mom likes to say our body smiles on the outside when we take care of it on the inside.

Here is the prayer that I started praying whenever I felt insecure (I still say this prayer if I ever have those feelings again):

Dear Heavenly Father,
Please help me love myself for so much more than my body.
Please help me see how beautiful I am. Help me to be confident when I feel insecure. Thank you, Lord, for making me so beautifully. I ask that you help all of the other people who are dealing with feelings of insecurities and self-consciousness.
Father, whenever they feel like they want to hide or cry because they don't look the way they want to, please let them remember how beautiful they are. I love you, Lord. In Your Holy Name, I pray,
Amen.

Mirror Reflection

List 10 things you love about yourself. (inner and/or outer)

1

2

3

4

5

6

7

8

9

10

Word Search

BEAUTY   DANCE   FOREVER   GIFT
CREATIVE   FUN   ADVICE   MERCY
SUN   FACE   ETERNAL   GRACE

LOOK UP, DOWN, & ACROSS FOR THESE WORDS

G	R	A	C	E	G	B	G	O	B
B	K	O	J	S	I	P	K	E	F
E	T	A	D	V	I	C	E	N	O
A	M	E	R	C	Y	U	C	J	R
U	C	S	V	G	I	F	T	P	E
T	F	U	N	Y	E	K	D	R	V
Y	K	C	R	E	A	T	I	V	E
D	F	A	C	E	C	F	Z	Y	R
M	S	U	N	E	T	Q	I	S	O
E	T	E	R	N	A	L	O	X	R

Day 13

jeal·ous

/ˈjeləs/ feeling or showing envy of someone
or their achievements and advantages

J ealousy is a feeling we don't want to admit.
God already knows. He always knows how you feel
so even before you admit it, he hears the jealousy in your
heart. Feeling jealous of someone is the same as hating on
God's blessing upon someone else's life. You may feel
jealousy in your heart and not even know it. A time where I
felt jealous is when I felt like my little sister didn't have to
work as hard as me. And I know what you're thinking…
that's something small; yes, it is, but at the same time, God
doesn't see jealousy on a spectrum. If you are jealous of
someone's new phone or jealous of someone's new house,
it is the same in God's eyes.

Being the oldest of three, I definitely have more
responsibilities. As a younger kid (9), I didn't understand
when my Mom and Dad would tell me to do things and my
sister could sit around. I felt jealous and wanted to be able
to do little tasks such as straightening up the couch or
restocking the tissue. Instead, I had to set the table and
vacuum. Now, of course, I know these are things that I
needed to learn how to do around the house to help my
parents but at such a young age, I felt like Cinderella!
Because of this, I would be mean to my sister because she

got easy jobs (I'm realizing that what I did was so silly, now that I'm telling you guys this story but hey, you live and you learn)! Sometimes we get jealous of others and forget to realize the good in life. Because you think someone is achieving in life, that isn't always the case. Don't ever let the thought of someone's accomplishments make you question yours. Everyone is an achiever, celebrate your achievements as they come.

Envy is also used interchangeably with jealousy. Envy is a feeling of discontent or resentment of someone else's possessions, qualities, or blessings. Envy is not of God as it distracts us from Him. We have the promise that if we delight in our heavenly Father, He will give us the desires of our hearts. So, remember to refocus your attention on Him and what He is doing in your life and not others. One way to get rid of jealousy is through prayer. After we've confessed to the Lord that we have jealous feelings, we must begin to pray for the other person.

James 4:11
"Brothers and sisters, do not slander one another. Anyone who speaks against a brother or sister or judges them speaks against the law and judges it. When you judge the law, you are not keeping it, but sitting in judgment on it."

Your prayer should consist of these five things: First, praise God for who He is. Secondly, confess your sins. Third, thank God. Fourth, pray for others. Fifth, pray for yourself.

Dear Lord,
Please help me be grateful for what I have. Please help me to
appreciate what you've blessed me with. Help me to
congratulate and celebrate with others instead of feeling
jealous of them. Thank you, Lord, for the blessings I have. I
ask that you help all of the other people who are dealing with
feelings of jealousy. Father, whenever I feel jealous please
remind me of everything I have. Allow me to remember how
blessed I am. I love you, Lord. In Your Holy Name, I pray,
Amen.

Mirror Reflection

List or draw some of the blessings in your life:

friend·ship

/'fren(d)SHip/ the emotions or conduct of
friends; the state of being friends

Friendships are so important in one's life. Sometimes in life, you go through experiences that you don't want to talk about to your Mom, Dad, sister, or anyone else. When you have these experiences, you sometimes may have friends around that you can talk to. But what happens when you struggle with finding friends you can trust?

All of my life I have struggled with keeping friendships and finding stable ones. I've been seen as an outcast by most people. They put me in the box of being "weird", "lame", or "a nerd". Now as a young child, those things hurt but as I've started to age and mature, those things don't really hurt me anymore. I've learned that being all the things they call me is what makes me stand out from the crowd. It's okay to be yourself If that's what makes you.

One specific time where I remember feeling like I was struggling to keep a friendship is my 10th-grade year of high school. I was good friends with a girl at school but when we would hang with each other outside of school, she'd try to get me to do things that she knows I'd never do. She'd try to peer pressure me into doing things that I knew would get me grounded by my parents. Luckily, I never let her get me to do the things. That friendship felt exhausting.

When she called, I didn't want to talk because the whole conversation would be about boys and gossip. She never wanted to talk about anything positive. She wanted me to live a YOLO (You Only Live Once) life. As Christians, living by the motto "YOLO" is a great thought, but we can YOLO and try to live in a way that doesn't get us grounded. I'm speaking to myself as well when I say this. I may not have done the things that my friend tried to get me to do, but I'm not an angel. I can't count how many times my parents have taken my phone. LOL

Over time, we stopped being as close and hanging out as much. I felt like a weight was lifted off of my shoulders. I felt bad for thinking of her like that but at the end of the day, you have to do what's good for yourself. Sometimes we think just because we only live once that it's okay to sneak out, drink illegally, or to do all of the things that make you stray away from God. If you are friends with someone you dread hanging out with or talking to, you should drop them for the good of yourself.

Sometimes we carry unnecessary burdens. Toxic friendships are often one of the many burdens that we allow to bring us down. We fall victim to naivety. If you feel like you have friendships that you need to drop, ask God about it. He will let you know what you need to do. Don't be afraid to talk to your parents. My parents actually spoke to me about this particular friend, but I didn't listen. I later began to see it for myself.

Matthew 5:30
And if your right-hand causes you to stumble, cut it off and throw it away. It is better for you to lose one part of your body than for your whole body to go into hell.

Dear God,
Thank You for allowing me to have good friends. Give me discernment as I heal from difficult friendships and choose new relationships. Please help me leave relationships that I'm struggling with and will have struggles with. Please help me to be a good friend, too. Help all of my brothers and sisters in Christ that don't know how to not fall victim to peer pressure. Help us be more like you Lord. In Jesus' Name,
Amen.

Mirror Reflection

Questions to ask yourself when identifying a good friend:

- Do I like who I am when I'm with them?
- Does it feel more like a job rather than a friendship?
- Does it feel right to you?
- Does their friendship represent your morals and values?

Betrayal
Matthew 6:14-15

be·tray·al

/bēˈtrāəl/ the breaking or violation of a
presumptive contract, trust, or confidence

Do you know how it feels to be betrayed? I do. Although strangers may reject, mock, or ridicule us, only those we love or trust can betray us, which makes it so painful. It hurts the most when they do it because of the relationship you once had. Imagine telling someone all of your deepest secrets and then they betray you by telling your business or using it against you. That relationship is altered once that level of trust is broken.

I've been betrayed many times in my life; sometimes by family, but mostly by friends. It was my freshman year of high school when I met this girl that radiated great energy.... or so I thought. One day we were talking about what we do outside of school and I told her about my vegan cosmetic line, BeYou+T. She was so amazed that I had a successful business, she even congratulated me on it and purchased one of my products. A few weeks later, she starts asking me all of these questions about why and how I started my business. I answered the questions truthfully because I didn't suspect that she was up to anything. After we finished the conversation, I went to the restroom. With me being a business owner and selling a product that girls my age like, I always bring products to sell at school and I keep them in a cute, small bag inside my backpack. When I came back, one of my friends asked me to purchase some, so I said sure! I went into my backpack to retrieve the product bag and guess what?! It was empty!

I know it couldn't have been anyone but her because it was full of products before I went to the restroom! I confronted her about it and she insisted that she didn't take it. It was too much product to let slide so I took it upon myself to tell my teacher. He made her empty her backpack and sure enough, all of the glosses she'd taken fell right out of her bookbag. I was so upset because I would never do something like that to her. The fact that she did it and we're in high school shows you that people will betray you no matter how old you are or how good of friends you think you guys are. It's up to you to forgive that person as Christ forgives you every day. You can forgive without still being friends. In this case, that is exactly what happened. It's ok to walk away from those who betray us, even if you have to work on the forgiving part.

Matthew 6:14-15
"For if you forgive other people when they sin against you, your heavenly Father will also forgive you. 15 But if you do not forgive others their sins, your Father will not forgive your sins."

Dear Heavenly Father,
Thank you for always forgiving me no matter what. As I
move forward with other friendships in my life, help me
not to punish those who have goodwill toward me by
assuming that they will betray me like people in the past
have done. Help me forgive others as you forgive me,
Lord. When I feel like giving up on friendships, Lord
please remind me that I will be okay and losing one friend
is not the end of the world. I ask that you please help any
of my brothers and sisters in Christ if they are going
through these same situations. I love you, Lord,
Amen.

Mirror Reflection

Process for forgiving others:

- Realize that your Father forgives you every day
- Understand that you make mistakes too.
- Do not hold a grudge against your brother or sister in Christ.

Please remember that forgiveness doesn't always happen overnight.

Standing Out

Jeremiah 1:5

Stand out

/stand/ /out/ to be easily seen or noticed

here is no denying that we live in a challenging time. We are living in an increasing world of scepticism. This is a difficult time for Christians, but a necessary one.

Before Jesus' death and resurrection, and after he had washed his disciples' feet, he told them: "A new command I give you: Love one another. As I have loved you, so you must love one another. 35 By this everyone will know that you are my disciples if you love one another." (John 13:34-35 NIV) Jesus also stated that by our love, all people will know that we are his disciples. So when the world chooses to show hate, we can choose to show love, just like our savior Jesus did. The world will begin to realize that we are different. We don't have to explain it, just be different. The more we become like our Saviour, the more different we will become from the world, and this is a beautiful thing. The world has its own way of thinking and living that we, as followers of Jesus, must avoid. However, we cannot transform ourselves. The work of God's Spirit within us must reprogram the corrupt mind that marks this world. Our lives change when we are changed from within.

For a Christian youth, the focus of life should not be on the "fitting in" but rather on the "standing out". Being different can be hard, but it can be done. "Standing out" produces character which assists in developing confidence.

Sometimes I still struggle with wanting to stand out. I tend to hide so I can fit in with the crowd and be "cool". That's a part of growing up though, wanting to be accepted. It's just human nature to want to be accepted by people but as I get closer to God, I notice that I start to care less and less about what the world thinks and more about what God thinks.

Jeremiah 1:5
"Before I formed you in the womb I knew[a] you before you were born I set you apart; I appointed you as a prophet to the nations."

Dear Heavenly Father,
I come to You in the name of Your Son, Jesus. I confess that I haven't lived my life for You. From this day forward, I'll live my life for You to the best of my ability. Help me to get past what others believe about me. Help me to believe what you believe about me.
In Jesus' Name, I pray,
Amen.

Mirror Reflection

It's great to be me! Everyone else is already taken.

One unique thing about me is...

I like who I am because...

I am natutrally gifted at...

Day 17

Identity in Christ
John 1:12

i·den·ti·ty

/ī'den(t)ədē/ the fact of being who or what a
person or thing is

As teenagers who are still trying to find out their own identity, it can be intimidating to find your identity in Christ.

So, what does identity in Christ mean? Collins Dictionary explains a person's identity as, "the characteristics that distinguish them from others." We are told that when we accept Christ into our hearts, the person we were before dies, and we are reborn as a "new creation." We lose our old identity and receive our new one, but what if you still feel the same after accepting Christ? I accepted Christ as my Lord and Savior at the age of 9 and was baptized. I remember that day so well. It was one of the best days of my life. A lot of my family members came to church that day to see me be baptized.

Being baptized was a feeling I can't describe. I was submerged. After going underwater and coming out again, I felt like the feeling I get on Christmas Day. Yes, it felt THAT good. The service was amazing and I was able to partake in Communion for the first time. I was beyond excited. I mean how could I not be? I was a "new creature", right? Well, when we returned home, we did our normal Sunday utine: Sunday dinner, watching a movie, and just hanging out. Later that evening, I got in trouble for something and it really confused me. How could I still be doing the same things I had done to get in trouble before being baptized? Did it not take?

I told my Mom about my concerns and she really opened my eyes. She said that we don't come to God and instantly become "good". We will forever be working on ourselves. Coming to Christ tells us and everyone else that I don't have it all together and that I know I will always need God to help me get it right.

We will fall but never stay there. Always get back up and try again. So, my baptism had "taken". Now I just have to keep moving forward in understanding who I am in Christ. As you and I both move forward in learning more about Jesus and having our own experiences, more and more of our identity in Christ will be shown to us.

John 1:12
"Yet to all who did receive him, to those who believed in his name, he gave the right to become children of God"

Dear Lord,
I pray that You would unlock my heart that I might be fully alive to my true identity in You. Help me to stand in Your truth against all enemy attacks and guard my heart with all vigilance. I thank You for my uniqueness and that I am made in Your image. I want to know You on a deeper level, and I don't want anything to hinder my relationship with You.
In Jesus' Name, I pray, Amen

Mirror Reflection

This activity may require you to talk with your Mom, Dad, Pastor, Sunday School teacher or anyone that helps you to understand how to find your identity in Christ.

I spend time with God by...

What is baptism?

One thing I want God to help me change is...

What does it mean to accept Christ?

What does Christ mean to me?

screen·time

/skrēn/ /tīm/ time spent using a device such
as a computer, television, or games console

In today's time, it's so easy to allow our screen time habits to get out of hand when we have so many channels of entertainment on the internet. As young Christians, we have to find a way to separate ourselves from worldly things like the media. Yes, it's hard, especially when you could scroll for hours like me but we have to create healthy screen time habits. I am not over my unhealthy screen time habits completely so for this devotion, I won't tell a story as I've done for the other devotions, but I will tell you how I'm creating better screen time habits.

When I could be studying or reading my bible, I'm scrolling on social apps or Facetiming with friends. Those are not bad things but we have to have a healthy balance between all things that we do. Doing our chores, homework, taking care of our siblings, taking care of ourselves, reading our Bible, etc., are all things that help us to be more responsible in our everyday lives. They help us to form healthy habits. Forming healthy habits in one area of your life will help you form healthy habits in another. A couple of things that I do to try to keep myself on track are:

- I set the timer on my phone for how long I will use a particular social media app and try my best not to start the time over. Usually, I set it in 10 minutes increments. I also set my timer when I'm reading my Bible or a devotional. I try to make this uninterrupted time by placing my phone on silent. No distractions! Each day I read for a longer amount of time and I get better at putting down my phone.

- Another way that I try to create healthy screen time habits is by paying attention to whom I follow online. I love following animal pages and seeing the crazy things that they do. I also love to follow anything that makes me laugh. I take the time to follow different Christian pages on social media, also. Every time that I see a Christian post I repost it and say a small prayer.

- My parents also monitor my screen time. Most nights, they set a time of when we should put our devices away for the night.

I think God appreciates the small gestures just as much as the big ones. I imagine creating healthy screen time habits puts a smile on His face.

Psalm 119:37
"Turn my eyes away from worthless things; preserve my life according to your word."

Most Gracious Heavenly Father,
Thank you for the good gift of the Internet and social media
through which we can create, communicate, learn, and glorify
you. I thank you for the ways you have blessed our world and
made lives easier because of the Internet and smart devices. I
praise you for giving the good gifts of creativity and work, and
that we can reflect your image online. I ask that when I let the
good gift you've given me replace you, you refocus my eyes on
what's important. I count it done in your name.
Amen.

Mirror Reflection

Pay attention to how much time you're spending on
social media and your devices. Use the space below to
write down 1 day of your social media or gaming use.
See where you're creating healthy screen time habits and
also look to see where you can improve.

Word Search

BOLD   HAPPY   FAMILY   STORY
LIFE   SUPER   WORLD   VERSE
FEAR   TRUTH   HEART   JESUS

LOOK UP, DOWN, & ACROSS FOR THESE WORDS

S	U	R	E	L	O	W	G	H	J
U	T	A	S	M	T	N	A	E	E
P	Y	O	R	Y	D	P	Q	A	S
E	B	Y	E	U	P	X	C	R	U
R	S	V	V	Y	B	M	Y	T	S
H	T	R	U	T	H	B	U	V	D
F	E	A	R	J	R	O	M	O	L
J	D	O	A	L	T	L	D	A	R
F	A	M	I	L	Y	D	H	Y	O
W	B	T	L	I	F	E	S	J	W

69

fo·cus

/ˈfōkəs/ pay particular attention to

Focus is something we need in every area of our life. I'm in the 11th grade and I was forced to do virtual school due to the Coronavirus outbreak. Going from being able to ask your teacher any question you had while at school to suddenly talking to them by typing on a keyboard is a big change. I am also a hands-on type of learner so school was actually fun for me when we got to do things that you can only do in school like Chemistry labs and playing competitive sports. The transition was hard and it still isn't easy as I sometimes struggle to get out of bed for my early morning classes. But as with anything else, you have to shift your mind to get used to our new normal. So I thought about other ways I've had to focus in life to help me become focused for virtual school.

Being focused can be difficult when you're surrounded by all of the distractions of the world, even the ones in your mind. It's hard to be focused on what's important in life and not the fun things but it has to be done. When I decided to start a business, there were many things that I had to focus on: what type of business it was going to be, what my products would look like, and then I had to focus on making the products. When I wanted to spend time on social media, I had to remember what's important. Devoting a specific time of the day to working on my business is how I got to where I am today. It was hard to put the phone down when I just wanted to spend my time scrolling and chatting. But when I look back at where I came from, it was worth it. I still have a lot more focusing to do and I continue to devote time to follow through with my plans of action. I know that I want to go to college, so I asked myself some of the same types of questions that I asked myself when starting my business to keep myself focused on virtual school. I asked myself, "What sort of grades do I want to make and what do I need to do to get there?". Writing a plan for virtual school the same way that I wrote a plan for my business has helped me to stay focused and to know when I get off track.

One thing about being focused is you can't just think that you're focused, you have to do the things that make you focused. It makes me think of the "Faith without works is dead" Bible verse (James 2:26). Believe it and then do it! Taking action always gets me focused.

Maybe you are starting a business or in the middle of a project, I've been there girl! Here are some tools to put your head on straight:

James 2:26
As the body without the spirit is dead, so faith without deeds is dead also

Dear Lord,
Please remove the distractions from my life. Please help me
and my brothers and sisters in Christ focus on the things we
need to get done. Help us focus on you as well Father so that
we are able to serve You better.
In Jesus' name, I pray,
Amen.

Mirror Reflection

The process of gaining focus:

1. Remove the distractions that you can remove i.e your phone or anything that you can control.
2. Put yourself first.
3. Devote a specific time of day to work on your plans
4. Evaluate periodically to make sure you're on the right track (like report cards)

● ●

What is one thing you can do today to get focused on achieving your current goal?

_____

_____

_____

_____

_____

_____

a·gape

/əˈgāp/ the highest form of love

My point for this devotional is to help you understand that even when you feel like no one around you loves you, God is always loving you, even if what's happening around you doesn't feel that way.

A specific time in my life when I felt unloved is when my parents were going through a separation. At the time, I was nine-years-old and I felt like my parents not being together was somehow my fault. It seemed that they were falling out of love with each other which made me feel like they might fall out of love with me. They didn't give me a reason to feel that way except that they were no longer together. Now that I'm older and I can look back on the situation, I understand that that wasn't the case at all. It's not that my parents no longer loved each other or no longer loved me but that we were going through hard times and needed God to help us to be a family again.

Every day I asked God why. "If you love me, then why would you let me go through this?". "If you love me, then why would you take my best friend [Dad] away?". Asking God all of these questions that I may never understand, especially at such a young age. It felt like God was punishing me because I can truly say that at nine-years-old,

73

that was one of the darkest times of my life. It was so hard for me because of the love I have for both my parents. I love them and everything about them being together. It made me happy seeing them smile when they would have conversations and play around and joke like married couples do. When all of that left my life for a split moment, I felt like love wasn't real. I began to believe that no one loved me, not even God because a God who loves me wouldn't put me through this much pain. You've seen me talk about this a lot throughout the book because God has been good to me and honestly I don't have a lot of sad stories to tell. My parents have been good to me, too. But this story has taught me the most about life, about myself, and mostly about who God is in my life.

As young Christians, we have to realize that God takes us on unexpected journeys. That doesn't mean he doesn't love us; he's just taking you on the journey he planned out for you before you were even born. "For God so loved the world, that He gave his only begotten son, that whosoever believeth in him should not perish, but have eternal life." [John 3:16] Think about that girl. He gave his ONLY begotten son for people like you and me. If that's not love, I don't know what is. We tend to forget all the ways God shows us love just because there are hardships in our life at the moment. He always pulls you through and keeps you afloat. He washes away your sins every day with the blood that Jesus Christ shed for us. We are made new every time we ask for forgiveness, no matter how many times we mess up. I tell you all of this to say that God loves you, no matter how you feel and no matter what you're going through. So the next time you feel unloved, remember the word "Agape" is the highest form of love that only God can and will give you.

1 John 4:16
"And so we know and rely on the love God has for us. God is love. Whoever lives in love lives in God, and God in them."

Dear Heavenly Father,
Thank You for Your never-failing love. Thank You for always being there even when I don't turn to you first for help. Thank You for carrying me when I couldn't go any more Lord. Thank You for everything you are about to do in my life that will overthrow everything I went through in the past.
In Your Holy Name, I pray,
Amen.

Mirror Reflection

Tips to help you know that God's love is amazing:

- Spend intentional quality time with the Lord. Read your Bible and confide in Him. He has all the love you will ever need.

- Love yourself. Just because you don't feel loved at the moment doesn't mean treat yourself like you don't love yourself.

- Do an activity that you enjoy doing. Go get your nails done, eat at your favorite restaurant, or get a new do!

- Always talk to your parents about your feelings if you have that type of relationship. If you don't, try your best to create it. God gave us the parents that we have for a reason. They are our special coaches from God. He gave them special thoughts to help guide us through good and bad times.

re·jec·tion

/rəˈjekSH(ə)n/ the dismissing or refusing of a
proposal or idea

I f there is one thing that can make someone feel like they don't have a friend in the world, it's rejection. Whether it be a teacher's insult, a friend's gossip, a boss's criticism, or a person who suddenly doesn't want to be seen with you anymore… rejection hurts at any age.

One time that I can remember experiencing rejection is when I tried out for my middle school's volleyball team. I worked hard that summer trying to gain the necessary skills to effectively be a volleyball team member. I went to conditioning and strength training all summer at the local recreation department. Try-outs rolled around and when the day actually came, I felt confident in my performance on the court. We got our results that night and to say the least, my results were disappointing. I didn't make the team but I was welcomed as a manager. After being cut from the team, it made me not want to be a part of it in any capacity. I realized that I have to work for what I want. If I wanted to get on the team, I had to take it little by little. I accepted my position as manager and while it wasn't what I wanted, I knew I had to be there in order to get where I wanted to go I spent the entire season as manager while still practicing by myself and sometimes with the team. I worked even harder than I did the first time. While pushing myself to the limit every day. I was so determined to make the team that I didn't care how much work I had to put in to lock in my spot on the team next year. I actually had fallen in love with volleyball. I'm not the athletic type which truly surprised me. It started off as a fun activity but then became a serious thing I wanted to pursue. The reason I was so determined is due to not earning a spot on the team, though I had worked so hard prior to trying out. After the season was over, I went right back to the local recreation department to continue to get better for next year's tryouts.

The conditioning season started and guess where I was? Out on the court and ready to show all my progress. I worked my butt off day in and day out. Tryouts rolled around again and guess what? I made the team after I put in all the hard work and effort to get there. Sometimes God makes you work a little harder to make sure you can handle what He's about to give you. Whenever you get rejected, take that as fuel to go harder in whatever it is you're trying to succeed at. God will help you through any obstacle. Always remember that. You still have to put in the work. One of my business besties, Gabby Goodwin, CEO of Confidence by Gabby, says it best. "No just means Next Opportunity." This can mean the next opportunity for you to try again or move on to something else. Only you can decide what it means to you.

Jeremiah 29:11
"For I know the thoughts that I think toward you, saith the Lord, thoughts of peace, and not of evil, to give you an expected end."

Dear Heavenly Father,
Thank you for giving me new opportunities. As I move forward in my life please help me realize that I can do all things through you. Help me to not give up when my problems feel so big and I feel so small. When I feel like giving up on things that are blocking my way, Lord please remind me that I will be okay, and losing or hearing a no one or more times is not the end of the world. I ask that you please help any of my brothers and sisters in Christ if they are going through these same situations. I love you, Lord,
Amen.

Mirror Reflection

Ways to overcome rejection:

- Refuse to Let Rejection Define You

- Learn From Rejection. Yes, rejection always teaches you a lesson, so dig deep to find it.

- Acknowledge your Emotions and MOVE ON!

stressed

/strest/ experiencing mental or emotional
strain or tension

In the midst of everything going on in the pandemic of 2020, me and my family experienced a tragic loss. My grandfather passed away due to COVID-19 complications. His death was so unexpected. We all had been social distancing and taking all the necessary precautions to stay safe.

Just when I thought life was going as good as it could get while being in a pandemic, life took a left turn. My whole world turned upside down in one phone call. My grandfather and I were so close and had an unbreakable bond. His passing was so unexpected and really broke me for a moment. I didn't want to get out of bed or do anything because everything made me think about him. I felt so numb and lost in my sadness. I took a week off from school to help my mental state. When I went back to school I had what seemed like 50 million assignments. I needed to take my time to grieve. When I felt like I was ready to get back to being somewhat normal again, I was bombarded with all of these assignments. I didn't know how I was going to do all of the assignments and the new assignments. My grades were starting to drop once the teachers put in the zeros and it just seemed like my life was crumbling down at once. Here I am 16 years old attending my junior year of high school online because of a global pandemic, dealing with the tragic loss of my grandfather, a lot of school assignments. To say that I was stressed was an understatement.

I spent my time sleeping, crying, eating, or catching up on assignments. For about three weeks, I hadn't talked to God about anything going on in my life. I was so focused on everything that I forgot about the main one keeping me afloat. One day, I picked up my bible and I just started reading. I didn't even know where to start. We can't lose sight of what's important during hard times. We can't forget about God when He is the main thing that can pull us out of stressful situations. I get it..sometimes it's hard to get up and pray or read your bible when all you want to do is sit and cry and feel down. I've been there and done that. Always remember that God can help you and He's there through everything, including the good and the bad times. There are also different services in place that can help you if you need professional counseling. God has given us experts to help talk us through grief. My church also has a grief support group that our lay shepherd made sure to remind us of during our time of bereavement.

Psalm 37:5
"Commit your way to the Lord; trust in him and he will do this."

Dear Heavenly Father,
We ask that when we become stressed that we seek out the help
we need in order to take the stress away. Help us to practice
good self-care and create healthy habits that help us to try to
keep stress at bay. Teach us how to continue to lay our cares on
the altar. Through your Spirit living in our hearts, give us
wisdom and strength. In Jesus' name, we pray.
Amen.

Mirror Reflection

Tips to relieve stress:

- Write down how you feel. Grab a journal or even write out your feelings in the notes app on your phone.
- Listen to Gospel music. When you feel like you can't get up and read your bible put on your favorite Christian jams and have a worship session.
- Talk to God. God is always listening and he hears you even when you're not talking. A simple prayer throughout the day can help you get closer to him in stressful times.
- Give yourself mental health days. My parents implemented mental health days in our family when we were little. My Mom said when she could see that school or anything was too much for us, she would let us stay home from school and one of my parents would take the day as well to make sure we were ok. Ask your parents about implementing those in your family.

peer pres·sure

/pi(ə)r ˈpreSHər/ influence from members of
one's peer group

I t can be easy to get caught up in peer pressure. When
you see your friends not making good decisions,
it can be really hard on you. You might feel pressured to go
along with them or to not make good choices too. In my
life, I have experienced plenty of peer pressure and I
probably will experience tons more.

One time I remember experiencing peer pressure was
when I was at school. Me and a group of friends were at
lunch sitting around the table having a good conversation.
One of our senior friends came to the table and asked if we
wanted to skip with them. They all said yes. I definitely
knew that it was a bad idea to do it for many reasons. I
would be skipping class, on the road with people that I
shouldn't be in the car with, and because I know who my
parents are and if they ever found out that I did something
like that… well, you know the rest. It was easy to say no
because there were more cons than pros in the situation.
Although it would've looked good that I was being
rebellious to my friends, the people that matter the most
would not approve of what they wanted me to do. They
kept begging and begging me to come with them but I just
couldn't take that risk, though I wanted to go, I said no.

In situations where there are a bunch of cons, it's easy to say no but what if there are more pros than cons..what should you do then? Think about what would Jesus do. Yes, I know it's very cliche but it helps keep you on track. Would Jesus smoke weed, sneak out, pop pills, or do anything of that sort? No, If he wouldn't, then neither should you. I get it, it's hard to not make worldly decisions because sometimes doing things that you aren't supposed to is fun... way more fun than following the rules and being the "goody-two-shoes" of the group. What we, as young Christians have to realize is every decision we make won't result in fun. The best reward is seeing those Golden streets in Heaven. Hearing "Well done my faithful servant" will be so worth it after saying no to all the bad decisions we wanted to make. When you're in a group and everyone else wants to do something that you know you're not supposed to do [be honest even if you want to do it, too] it's ok to say no. You don't have to explain it or anything. There may be someone in the group just waiting on someone else to say no because they can't say it.

Peer pressure controls all of us from time to time. We want to be accepted, approved of, and popular. Sometimes it's hard being different and we allow ourselves to be shaped by people's opinions rather than by what God wants for us. When we notice that we are making more bad decisions than good ones, recognize and change them. Just because you start to go down a bad road doesn't mean you can't turn around and go down a different road.

Proverbs 1:10
"My son, if sinful men entice you, do not give in to them."

Dear God,
I'm starting to find myself making bad decisions. I need to get back on the right track. Please help me to stand up for what's right and if that means standing alone, please help me deal with that feeling. I am learning that my thoughts create my experiences and whatever I experience on the outside is a projection of what I am thinking on the inside. Please help me think in ways and surround myself with people that are beneficial to me. In Your name, I pray,
Amen.

Mirror Reflection

In the space below, please write your best advice for a friend who is dealing with peer pressure?

_____
_____
_____
_____
_____
_____
_____
_____
_____

drugs

/drəg/ any substance which, when taken into the body,
alters the body's function either physically and/or
psychologically. Drugs may be legal or illegal

Some teens and tweens eagerly experiment with new drugs, frequently combining them with alcohol. I do not use drugs but I know a few people that do. Adults and teens, and tweens. Research shows that substance abuse and depression go hand in hand. And, conversely, depression increases the risk of substance abuse. Here's how: All drugs of abuse, including alcohol, act upon the same area of the brain involved in the regulation of mood. Experimentation with drugs or alcohol alters the balance of neurotransmitters (brain chemicals) in this part of the brain. Regular use of mind-altering drugs such as marijuana, cocaine, and alcohol cause temporary surges in these neurotransmitters resulting in a short-lived "high." Some people claim that they use drugs to enhance their spirituality. I'm not sure how that works, but make sure you're not experimenting with it. I have not heard my parents or my Pastor say anything about using drugs to speak to God.

If you are depressed or abusing drugs or alcohol, please know that you will get over it because these problems are very treatable. Sometimes bad habits are hard to quit, so make sure you understand the consequences of drug use. Don't even start. Don't be afraid to learn about it because it might just be you who saves a friend or a loved one from the struggles of drug use. I remember being a part of the D.A.R.E. Program in school. The police officer showed us the different types of drugs and gave us ways to say no to drugs. If you are experiencing peer pressure to try drugs or already using drugs, talk with someone who will listen and be honest with you like a parent, trusted friend, pastor, or family doctor. Treatment usually involves counseling, medication, and 12 step meetings. Whatever it takes–do it. Your life is precious and God has a purpose and plan for you that does not include drugs. Self-care goes much further than what we do to the outside of our bodies. It also is what we put inside of our bodies. We have to take care of our temple.

1 Corinthians 6:19-20
"Do you not know that your bodies are temples of the Holy Spirit, who is in you, whom you have received from God? You are not your own; 20 you were bought at a price. Therefore honor God with your bodies."

Dear Lord Jesus Christ,
Please help us to not start using drugs at any part of our lives.
When we find that things are tough, please allow us to turn to
you or our loved ones instead of drugs for comfort. If we come
into contact with drugs, please give us the strength to say no
and walk away from making a bad decision. And for our
friends that may be using drugs, Lord we ask that you help
them to stop. In Jesus's name, I pray,
Amen!

Mirror Reflection

Here is a list of resources that you and your friends can
use to learn how and why we should say no to drugs.

What You Need to Know About Drugs
kidshealth.org/en/kids/know-drugs.html

Smoking Stinks!
kidsHealth.org/en/kids/smoking.html

What Kids Say About: Drinking Alcohol
kidsHealth.org/en/kids/poll-alcohol.html

The D.A.R.E. Program
dare.org

Outsmart the Chart
scholastic.com/headsup/pdfs/NIDA2-
AB%20worksheet_p14.pdf

Say No to Drugs Flyer

After you've looked at the resources on the previous page, use the space below to create a flyer that tells your peers to say no to drugs. Be creative!

de·pressed

/dəˈprest/ (of a person) in a state of general
unhappiness or despondency

People often think that because we are young, we
can't be depressed. This is not true! I'm not talking
about being clinically depressed, even though that happens,
too. I'm talking about those times when something makes
us sad, stressed, or we can't stop worrying about it. Those
things make us depressed, too. The goal is to not get
depressed, but when you find yourself in a state of
depression, how do we get out of it?

When I was in 7th grade, I was going through a self-
identity crisis and dealing with insecurities, which caused
me to be depressed. Depression is real and can be crucial to
our lives. I was so insecure about things which led me to
depression. I felt weird, unwanted, and like an outkast in
friend groups. It wasn't a good feeling. I would cry and cry
but that didn't change anything. What truly helped me to
change was learning ways to destress, be secure in my own
skin, and taking life one day at a time. Never feel that what
you're feeling is not a big enough problem to speak to
someone about. If it's bothering you, it's bothering you for a
reason, so find a way to deal with it so that you won't
become depressed.

Deuteronomy 31:8
"The Lord himself goes before you and will be with you;
he will never leave you nor forsake you. Do not be afraid;
do not be discouraged."

Dear Lord,
There are times when we get depressed about something we
may be dealing with or someone close to us may be dealing
with. Help us to shake ourselves out of it. Place the right people
in our lives to help see when we need a friend to talk to when
we try to hold it all in. Help us to use the tools you and our
parents have given us in order to not get depressed, but when
we find that we are that we run to you and them to seek
guidance. In Jesus' name, I pray,
Amen.

Mirror Reflection

Self Care Tips to help you shake yourself out of a
depressed state.

- Take good care of yourself. If you need to take self-
  care days, then do that.
- Go to the spa, get a mani & pedi, a massage, or a
  facial, whatever you do make sure it makes you feel
  good :)
- Find ways to handle your stress i.e., (finding
  hobbies, exercising)
- Find someone to confide in, whether it's friends or
  family. Make sure you trust them.

en·cour·age

/in'kərij/ give support, confidence, or hope to
(someone)

It's so easy to feel discouraged. Laziness and procrastination play big parts in feeling discouraged. Laziness is the unwillingness to work or use energy. Procrastination is the act of delaying or postponing something. Sometimes we feel like we can't do it when you actually can! Our biggest enemy is ourselves. We must encourage ourselves. Oftentimes, we get into our heads and convince ourselves that we can't do it, not smart enough, good enough, skilled enough, or pretty enough which is NOT the case! When you speak like that to yourself you get discouraged and allow laziness and procrastination to set in can do anything you put your mind to.

A time when I needed to encourage myself was in 5th grade. I entered a kids' cooking contest. You had to formulate a kid-friendly recipe for an after school snack. My mom and I worked all afternoon thinking of the perfect recipe. After we decided on the perfect idea, I packed up my entry form and couldn't wait to turn it in at school the next day. I turned it in and I was registered. With the contest only a week and a half away, I kept thinking of all the negative outcomes. "What if I don't win?". "What if the judges don't like my recipe?", "What if I get nervous and make it incorrectly?".

I was filling my head with so much negativity that I was starting to become discouraged before the contest even started. The days flew by and it was finally time to whip up my recipe for the judges. I went to my station and everything I needed had already been laid out. I even had an adult assistant! I felt like I was on one of those cooking shows I always watch when I should be asleep! I looked around the room and I saw that everyone else's stations were all decked out with decorations, balloons, and lots of cool things. They even had much more ingredients than I did. The excitement went away and negativity filled all my thoughts. A wave of nervousness came over me and it was bad. I was so nervous to the point where my hands were getting all sweaty and shaky. The time for the contest to start rolls around and they tell us that we have 40 minutes to create our dish. I was so nervous but I said to myself, "I know you can do it, you got this." So I went to work putting together my dish, making sure it was perfectly plated.

The five-minute mark rolled around and I'm looking at kids' dishes and they looked amazing! The judges came around, tasted, and rated all of the dishes. They got to my table and as I hoped, they loved my dish! It met all of the requirements for the contest. It was kid-friendly, tasty, and the perfect afternoon snack! They were thoroughly impressed with what I had created. I couldn't have been happier because I was so worried about them not liking it. After tasting everyone's dishes, they went back to the judges' station to score them. They took 30 minutes to complete scores which felt like forever. When they were done, they called all the contestants up to the stage. I was literally scared. They started calling out the winners. Third place, not me. Second Place, not me. I started to lose hope. They did a drumroll… "The first place winner is…*dead silence pierces my heart* JASIYA GREEN!"

I jumped up so big and proud. I honestly didn't think I could do it but this goes to show you that we are our biggest enemy. We get into our heads and fill it up with negative thoughts but in reality, you can do it! You can do anything you put your mind to, especially when you put your faith in the Lord. Don't allow laziness and procrastination to set in. When it was time to enter the contest, I went straight to working on a recipe and entered the contest. What if I had waited and missed the deadline? I could have missed a wonderful opportunity. What if I hadn't encouraged myself? Even if you don't believe it at the time, try your very best and encourage yourself to think that you can and you will!

2 Corinthians 13:14
"May the grace of the Lord Jesus Christ, and the love of God, and the fellowship of the Holy Spirit be with you all."

Dear Heavenly Father,
Please help us to encourage ourselves when we think we can't do something or lack the confidence to try. Help us combat intimidation, laziness, and procrastination so that we don't miss the great opportunities that you have for us.
In Jesus' name I pray,
Amen.

Mirror Reflection

Use the quote bubbles below to encourage yourself. How would you tell yourself, "You Can Do It?"

ac·cept·ance

/ək'septəns/ the action or process of being
received as adequate or suitable, typically to
be admitted into a group

Most of us are driven to be accepted. Whether it's
acceptance from a group of students at school,
your parents, or maybe even at a job, our need for
acceptance is strong and it's human nature. When you don't
feel accepted, it can shake your confidence. It can make
you fear others or certain situations. Part of not letting your
confidence get shaken by the actions of others is realizing
that you're always accepted by God.

There are many times in my life where I wanted to feel
accepted at school and home or just in general. I never
wanted to feel like an outcast or the odd one, but sometimes
I did. As a young Christian, we may struggle with choosing
God or the world as I know I do. I was so bent on worrying
about who likes me or wants me around rather than what
God wants. I wanted to change my appearance and attitude
just to be accepted. I want you to remember that you are
accepted by God and outside of Him, it doesn't matter if
you're accepted or not. The hard part for us is really
believing that truth. It's easy to let our feelings and hurts
from rejection be more real to us than the fact that in Christ
we're accepted. So if you struggle with rejection and hurt,

begin to think about this scripture:

Psalm 18:19
"He brought me out into a spacious place; he rescued me because he delighted in me."

    Realize that there is power in seeing yourself as God sees you. He wants you on his team. Disregard anyone who makes you feel left out and leaves you begging for their acceptance. It's not worth changing yourself for them. Be yourself and shine from within! Your beauty is unique to you, so don't change it for the approval of others.

Dear Gracious and Loving God,
As I take this time to be still, help me to let go of anxiousness and feel your peace. Your Word says that you are love and where there is love there can be no fear. Help me to let go of fear and receive your perfect love. I come before you with heaviness because of being hurt by others. Help me to accept the effect that their actions have had in my life and to let go of this hurt. I accept and find comfort in knowing—I am completely loved with your divine, perfect love. In the name of your Son whose example lights our way,
Amen

Mirror Reflection

YOU are special to God. YOU are made in his image. We should view ourselves as loved and precious and treat others with more love if we truly believe we were each made in God's image. We're all different, but each of us represents God. Please place your favorite photo of you in the space below. Each time you look at it, I pray that it is a reminder that you should accept yourself and others as God has accepted us even with all of our inner and outer differences.

Coloring Fun

bul·ly

/'boŏolē/ seek to harm, intimidate, or coerce

In life, you will run into people that let you down and disappoint you. Sometimes people don't say or do the right thing. Perhaps they have bullied you or treated you unkindly. What do you do in situations like these when people aren't treating you with the respect and care you feel you deserve?

In my life, I'm not going to necessarily say I've been bullied but I have been picked on a lot for things that I can't change about myself. One thing about people that pick on you a lot is there is something about them that they don't like, so they put the attention on you. People that truly love themselves don't bully others. Sometimes it's obvious the bully has some serious issues and is in need of help. I'm sure you want them to get that help or at the very least, you want them to leave you alone. We know that God doesn't like us to bully one another.

No matter what a mean person has done to you or how bad someone might have hurt you, you still have the responsibility to respond back to them in love. The good news is that God will help you out by giving you the love to do it. It's just up to you to believe it and tap into that love that is inside of you. Loving mean people can be hard, but with God's help, you can do it!

Leviticus 19:18
"Do not seek revenge or bear a grudge against anyone among your people, but love your neighbor as yourself. I am the Lord."

Dear Heavenly Father,
Your Word says that we are to treat people in the way that we want to be treated. We confess that we will practice this command and be kind and fair. We will be good friends and tell an adult when someone is being mean to another person. We will try our best not to push, shove, or fight. We declare that You, Lord will be the light and salvation for those who are being bullied and mistreated so they will not have to be afraid. We declare that You will cause the bad people who go around bullying people to fail in their actions. We confess that Your angels will protect those people who are being bullied wherever they go. We declare that You will rescue those who love You and will protect those who trust in You.
In Jesus's name I pray,
Amen

Mirror Reflection

What is considered bullying?

- Teasing
- Name-calling
- Inappropriate sexual comments
- Taunting
- Threatening to cause harm
- Physical or verbal abuse

Have you ever stood up for someone being bullied? Who was it? What was the bully doing? What made you defend the person being bullied?

_____

_____

_____

_____

_____

What does cyberbullying look like? Is it different from "traditional" bullying, and if so, how?

_____

_____

_____

You're Worth Waiting For
Colossians 1:11

wait·ing

/ˈwādiNG/ the action of staying where one is
or delaying action until a particular time

Waiting. It's one word with a big impact. It requires patience and discipline. You have to will yourself to do so, even if you don't want to. Our parents may tell us to wait to do this or that and we don't understand why. We just want to do whatever it is. Sometimes it could be something fun but dangerous like trying to get on the fastest roller coaster at an amusement park when you're five but you're not old or tall enough. You have to wait until the time is right. Dating is one of those things we may have to wait on in our tween and teen years until we're ready and our parents allow it.

Boys have been on my radar since middle school but of course, my parents were not about to let me have a boyfriend at that time. They did allow me to have a "special guy friend". My parents explained boy/girl relationships are important at any stage in our lives because they help us to learn from each other. Being romanticly involved with someone before you're ready can teach you too much too fast. So my parents had "the talk" with me. We discussed why they wanted me to wait for a "boyfriend" and we even talked about when they would allow it. The magic age of

16. Some people may think it's weird to talk to your Mom and Dad about stuff like that but who would be better to talk to about it? I asked questions and they answered. What I liked most about our conversation is why they told me that I should wait. It wasn't a yelling match or a no you can't do this. It was more "we want you to wait because...". I love that about my parents. They allow us to talk to them about anything and not judge us for it. They are stricter than most of my friends' parents, but at the same time they give me reasons (even if I don't like them) and not just say, "because I said so."

The point that I'd like to make here is that you can wait to have a boyfriend even if all of your friends have one. Trust me, I know it's hard especially when you like someone and they like you back. Waiting to have a boyfriend has allowed me to stay focused on what's the main thing right now: school, family, my business, and God. It's also nice to have a "special guy friend." The important thing is you have to know when you're ready and of course talk to your parents about it, but know that you're worth waiting for. Boys can wait!

Colossians 1:11
"Being strengthened with all power according to his glorious might so that you may have great endurance and patience."

Dear Lord,

Thank you for parents that guide me to make tough decisions when I'm not ready to make them yet. Please allow me to have patience and to discipline myself when it is needed. Thank you for friendships with the opposite sex so that we can learn from one another and enjoy each other in a Godly manner. Lord, I thank you for the conversations this devotion will open up between parents and children as they talk about major boyfriend/girlfriend relationships. Please help each of them to have an understanding of what you're worth waiting for means to them. In Jesus' name, I pray,

Amen.

Mirror Reflection

Tips for dating:

- Be yourself in the relationship.

- Make sure the person you're with brings out the best in you.

- Set appropriate boundaries so you can be comfortable in the relationship.

be·you

/bē/ /yo͞o,yə/ the state of becoming who God
has made you to be flaws and all

How many times have you heard someone say, "Just be you"? I've heard it a million times and now I'm going to say it to you. Just be you! During these thirty days, we've talked a lot about what God wants. We've talked about how to be God's girl and live in a way that glorifies Him, but I just want to make it plain and simple that He just wants you to be you. That's right. No hidden messages. Nobody else, just you. YOU ARE ENOUGH! YOU ARE AMAZING! Perfection is NEVER the goal because we can't achieve it, but we have access to a perfect God who makes all things new; even us.

God is our flashlight through life, shining the light on our paths. Sometimes we make take the wrong road, but we can't beat ourselves up about it. No matter how many times we get on the wrong track always get back on track so that you can find all the treasures that He has waiting for us. My first lipgloss that I learned to make was plain lipgloss with only essential oils, no flavoring. I wanted it to be one of my signature glosses because sometimes we don't need all the extra to just Be You and that's what I named it as a reminder to myself and to other girls. Being you is

EVERYTHING it's cracked up to be. Think about it for a second. There's no blueprint to being you because there wasn't a "you" created until you were created. Isn't that the cool thing about Go? He lets us be the first and only one to be ourselves. There's no way to mess it up. As tweens and teens, we're still learning who we are and who we're called to be so give yourself some Grace and just Be You!

Jeremiah 29:11
"For I know the plans I have for you," declares the Lord, "plans to prosper you and not to harm you, plans to give you hope and a future."

Dear Heavenly Father,
Teach us how to be ourselves. Help us to be okay with being who you created us to be. While we're on this journey of self-love and self-discovery lead us to those who you would have to teach us right from wrong. Help us to stay on the right path, but be brave enough to say when we need help doing so. Thank you for creating me in your image.
In Jesus' name, I pray,
Amen

Love Note to Yourself

What loving advice do you want to give to yourself 5 years from today? Encourage yourself. Speak life to yourself.

Today's date_____

How old are you now?_____

How old will you be in 5 years?_____

_____

_____

_____

_____

_____

_____

_____

_____

_____

_____

_____

_____

_____

_____

Girl's Night In

Girl's Night In is a celebration my Mom came up with when I was a little girl. Usually, we have them on a Friday night so we call it Friday Night In. We have so much fun. We have girl talk and do at-home spa treatments like doing our nails, face masks, and have food and cucumber water. As the years have gone by, our girl talks have become more intense as we have discussed several of the topics discussed in this devotional.

What I love most about Girl's Night In is spending quality time with my Mom and little sister. Sometimes we have guests (my girl cousins, friends, and even my grandmas). I'm sharing this tradition with you so that you can either start a self-care tradition with your Mom or take the time to see what you can begin to add to your Mother-Daughter time. Over the years, we've added devotional time and journaling. You don't have to do all of the activities in one night. You pick and choose a few and you set the time limit. Trust me. It's fun! If you create a Girl's Night In, share your photos on social media and be sure to tag @beyouplust. We'd love to see your photos!

Self-Care Tips Using Things Found in Your Kitchen

Being confident within helps us to be confident on the outside. We have to take care of our inner selves and outer selves. As a beauty brand CEO of a vegan cosmetic line, I wanted to show you how to use non-toxic items for your at-home self-care. In the next few pages, you will find ways to self-care at home using things you can find in your kitchen.

Disclaimer
Be sure to ask your parents before using these recipes. BeYou+T Cosmetics and its affiliates should not be held liable for any adverse reactions. Try these at your own risks.

5 Ways to Take Care of Your Lips

When it comes to your lips, don't slack off during the cooler months. Here are 5 ways to take care of your lips to make sure they don't crack but stay hydrated and moisturized.

Exfoliate.
Exfoliating your lips can help eliminate some of the dry, flaking skin that build-up and immediately restore shine, softness, and smoothness to your lips. You should exfoliate your lips 2-3 times per week. Some recommend every day, but you have to be mindful of what works for you.

Hydrate.
Hydrate your lips and your body. Drink the recommended amount of water for your body size. Hydrating your body helps to hydrate your lips and other parts of your body. It also helps you to have clear skin.

Protect and moisturize.
You want to use lip gloss, lip balm, and sugar scrub that will replenish moisture in your lips. Using essential oils in BeYou+T Cosmetic lip items helps with retaining moisture in your lips. This also helps to protect your lips from cracking.

Reapply often.
You want to purchase lip gloss, lip balm, and other lip items that you don't have to reapply like every 10 minutes. You want to make sure you're reapplying as often as needed. BeYou+T Cosmetic lip glosses and lip balm are long-lasting.

Use the right products. (No YUCKY stuff)
You want to make sure that you can pronounce the names of the ingredients of the items you're using on your lips (and body). You should be using items that are not harsh to your skin. Did you know that your skin is the largest organ on your body?

Our lip care kit will help you do all 5!!! It's also one of our best sellers! Scan the bar code below to grab yours today!

SCAN ME

Simple Sugar Scrub Recipe

This simple DIY sugar scrub exfoliates and moisturizes all at once. Massage a small amount into your skin or lips in circular motions for 20 seconds. Rinse with water and gently pat dry. Your skin will feel brand new and incredibly soft and luxurious.

Ingredients

- 1/4 cup sugar
- 1 teaspoon olive oil
- 5 drops vanilla flavoring
- 1/2 cup coconut oil

Simple Turmeric Masks for Gorgeous, Glowing Skin Recipe

Turmeric offers internal and external benefits. There are plenty of ways to incorporate its healing properties into your beauty routine. One way to do that is by using it in a face mask.

Ingredients

- 2 tablespoons of flour
- 1 teaspoon turmeric
- 3 tablespoons milk
- A few drops of honey

Mix flour, turmeric, honey, and milk to make a paste. Apply a thin layer to your face and let it dry for 20 minutes. Rinse off in the shower or at the sink, scrubbing gently to remove. Apply your favorite moisturizer. Grapeseed oil is a great moisturizer.

Home Remedy To Help You Deal With Dark Underarms

Many things can make your underarm become darker. Here's a non-toxic way to brighten them overtime.

Ingredients

- 1 lemon

Cut the lemon in half. Rub the lemon across your underarms. You can let sit for 15-30 minutes or you can sleep with it on. Be sure to wash your underarms thoroughly after it sits your desired amount of time.

Meet the Author

Jasiya "Jojo" Green
is the 16-year-old founder and CEO of BeYou+T
Cosmetics, a vegan skincare line. Her mission is to
empower girls from within while also teaching why and
how to use non-toxic beauty products for self-care needs.
She is also the CEO & Founder of Jojo's PersonaliTV. She
currently resides in South Carolina with her parents, Jason
and Tamell Green, her sister, Jakayla Green, and her
brother, Jason Green, Jr., AKA JJ. To learn more about
Jasiya, please visit her website at **beyouplust.com** or
jasiyagreen.com.

CPSIA information can be obtained
at www.ICGtesting.com
Printed in the USA
LVHW010145230221
679611LV00002B/116

9 781736 367490